M000233526

NONE *of* THESE THINGS MOVE ME

STANDING FIRM IN THE MIDST OF TRIALS

DON MCCLURE

CALVARY CHAPEL PUBLISHING
SANTA ANA, CALIFORNIA

None of These Things Move Me
Standing Firm in the Midst of Trials

Copyright © 2004 by Don McClure

Published by Calvary Chapel Publishing (CCP)
a resource ministry of Calvary Chapel of Costa Mesa
3800 South Fairview Rd.
Santa Ana, CA 92704

Second printing, 2004
First printing, 2003

ISBN 1-931667-73-X

Photography by Jean Guichard / © Jean Guichard / AlphaPix.com

Printed in the United States of America

CONTENTS

INTRODUCTION

And now, behold I go bound in spirit unto Jerusalem, not knowing the things that shall befall me there: save that the Holy Ghost witnesseth in every city, saying that bonds and afflictions abide me. But none of these things move me, neither count I my life dear unto myself, so that I might finish my course with joy, and the ministry, which I have received of the Lord Jesus, to testify the gospel of the grace of God.

—Acts 20:22–24, KJV

My Life Verse

IT was a rainy December night in 1966 when Acts 20:22-24 came home to me in a personal and powerful way. I had a little white convertible, a Triumph Spitfire, that weighed 1,440 pounds. That night, I was driving down the main street in Pasadena, California, when, unbeknownst to me, a drunk driver came barreling toward me from the other direction in a 1959 Oldsmobile 98, a rather large vehicle. (I think most of them are over in

1

Europe now, being used as tanks!) They are massive hunks of steel that own the road.

Well, the driver of this tank decided he didn't like his side of the road, so he veered over onto mine, and we had a horrible head-on collision. He flew forward into his steering wheel, and although he wasn't feeling any pain, he stumbled from his car with a bloody face. The Oldsmobile may have gotten a nick on the bumper. On the other hand, my little sports car was demolished; the engine was shoved back into the passenger compartment and it was on fire. I should have been killed, but instead I got out of that wreck without so much as a scratch. I was in a daze, though; to this day, I don't even remember getting out of the car.

It was a spectacular crash and rescue personnel raced to the scene. The police officer that questioned me refused to believe I had escaped from the pile of burning steel in the road. He looked at the car, looked at me, and then actually asked where the body was! When I told him I was the driver, he barked, "This isn't a joking matter, I want to know where that body is!" Eventually he believed me, so he ordered me to sit down. I was in shock, but felt fine; I didn't even want to go to the hospital. Still, I obeyed him and sat down on the curb. When I looked up, I saw my mother and sister walking down the sidewalk weeping because they thought I was dead. It was a heart-wrenching sight. We all realized what a miracle it was that I had survived. Some people have traumatic events that have no effect on their lives or that have a short-term effect, but that car accident was the catalyst for a radical change in my life.

Up until that night, I had been living a worldly life. My parents and siblings had all come to the Lord, but I had been sort of the black sheep of the family until one day my dad came to me with a request. He said, "Your mom would like you to go with us to the Billy Graham Crusade at the L.A. Coliseum." I hemmed and hawed, but when he reminded me how little my mother asked of me, I reluctantly agreed to go with them. As Billy Graham preached the simple Gospel message, everyone else in the arena seemed to disappear, and his words burrowed deep into my heart, convincing me that I was a sinner in need of a Savior. When he gave the invitation, I was out of my seat in a flash. I didn't even think to tell my parents that I would meet them in the parking lot afterwards.

The intensity of that moment soon faded though, and because there was no follow-up, I didn't grow in the Lord. I believed with all my heart that the Bible was true and that my sins were forgiven because of Jesus' death and resurrection, but my spiritual life was terribly unstable. If I was at church, I was moved spiritually and I could fit in. (I usually ate a lot of breath mints before I went because I smoked and I thought, "Well, you're not supposed to smoke, I don't think, until you get to hell.") But then I'd go back to college where most of my friends were in the fraternity and into the party scene, and I would be *moved* right back again. It was a cycle I hadn't been able to break out of.

But that night after the accident, everything in my life came to a screeching halt and I surrendered to the Lord. Alone in my bedroom and grateful to be alive, I got down on my knees and prayed, "God, I don't know what it means, but I'm Yours." Then I opened my Bible and began reading into the early hours of the morning. The Scriptures sprang to life when I read a story from the life of Paul in Acts, chapter 20.

I didn't know anything about Acts or the Apostle Paul, I knew nothing of Ephesus, and I really didn't even understand the passage I was reading. But when I came across Paul's bold statement: "None of these things move me" in verse 24, the words hit me like a ton of bricks, and I found myself envious of the Apostle Paul. Here was a man who could say, "Nothing moves me. I'm fixed. I'm unchangeable. I am what I am day and night, coming or going, up or down." As an ambitious college student, I cared tremendously about where I was going. I was planning to become a businessman like my father and my grandfather, who had established the first escrow company in California. My dreams were geared towards earning a lot of money and playing golf every chance I got. But here was Paul, who, instead of being ambitious, didn't seem to care about his life or future at all. I marveled at that and thought, "Wouldn't it be something, not to be moved?"

I was so completely taken by Paul's words that I immediately memorized Acts 20:24 and made it my life verse. I quoted it to people and even signed all my correspondence "Don McClure, Acts 20:24." This signified an authentic transformation, but it wasn't long before I was forced to decide whether or not I actually intended to live by those words, and the journey toward emulating Paul's majestic faith began.

APPLICATION & EXHORTATION

1. Are you easily moved by friends, circumstances, or your environment?

———※———

So you shall not turn aside from any of the words which I command you this day, to the right or the left, to go after other gods to serve them.

—Deuteronomy 28:14

For do I now persuade men, or God? Or do I seek to please men? For if I still pleased men, I would not be a bondservant of Christ.

—Galatians 1:10

Beware, brethren, lest there be in any of you an evil heart of unbelief in departing from the living God; but exhort one another daily, while it is called "Today," lest any of you be hardened through the deceitfulness of sin. For we have become partakers of Christ if we hold the beginning of our confidence steadfast to the end.

—Hebrews 3:13–14

2. Do the Scriptures spring to life when you read them or do they seem dull and confusing?

———— ❧☙ ————

The law of the LORD is perfect, converting the soul; the testimony of the LORD is sure, making wise the simple; the statutes of the LORD are right, rejoicing the heart; the commandment of the LORD is pure, enlightening the eyes.

—Psalm 19:7–8

The earth, O LORD, is full of Your mercy; teach me Your statutes ... great are Your tender mercies, O LORD; revive me according to Your judgments.

—Psalm 119:64,156

For the word of God is living and powerful, and sharper than any two-edged sword, piercing even to the division of soul and spirit, and of joints and marrow, and is a discerner of the thoughts and intents of the heart.

—Hebrews 4:12

3. Have you surrendered your life to the Lord? If not, what are you waiting for?

I call heaven and earth as witnesses today against you, that I have set before you life and death, blessing and cursing; therefore choose life, that both you and your descendants may live; that you may love the LORD your God, that you may obey His voice, and that you may cling to Him, for He is your life and the length of your days; and that you may dwell in the land which the LORD swore to your fathers, to Abraham, Isaac, and Jacob, to give them.

—Deuteronomy 30:19–20

Come to Me, all you who labor and are heavy laden, and I will give you rest.

—Matthew 11:28

As many as I love, I rebuke and chasten. Therefore be zealous and repent.

—Revelation 3:19

Chapter One

THE KEY TO A MAJESTIC FAITH

THE Apostle Paul is perhaps the greatest example from Scripture of one who lived triumphantly in the midst of the harshest of realities. I have always loved Paul's teaching, but a faith like his has always seemed out of reach to me. I've never identified with him as much as the more obviously flawed characters in the Bible—people like David who, despite his love for God, committed adultery and murder; or Moses, who lost his temper and was not permitted to go into the Promised Land.

The summits Paul reached seem more attainable once we understand a simple fact that distinguishes him from ordinary men: Paul knew how to handle a trial. Isn't it when a trial comes that our faith wavers and all our platitudes evaporate? Why is that? To some degree, it is because we are part of a generation that is unprepared for suffering. Everything about our environment and culture tells us that pain is an enemy to be avoided at all costs. So we easily get thrown off course spiritually when things don't go our way. But reading the New Testament, we find that when the early Christians surrendered their lives to Jesus Christ, one thing was assured: trials and persecution would follow. It was only a matter of when and how often. They lived with the expectation of suffering.

In 2 Corinthians 11:23–28, Paul paints a picture of the Christian life that is nearly unimaginable to the modern Western mind. Defending himself against the accusations of false brethren, he says,

Are they ministers of Christ?—I speak as a fool—I am more: in labors more abundant, in stripes above measure, in prisons more frequently, in deaths often. From the Jews five times I received forty stripes minus one. Three times I was beaten with rods; once I was stoned; three times I was shipwrecked; a night and a day I have spent in the deep; in journeys often, in perils of waters, in perils of robbers, in perils of my own countrymen, in perils of the Gentiles, in perils in the city, in perils in the wilderness, in perils in the sea, in perils among false brethren; in weariness and toil, in sleeplessness often, in hunger and thirst, in fastings often, in cold and in nakedness—besides the other things, what comes upon me daily: my deep concern for all the churches.

We know nothing of this type of suffering; and, we often don't even know how to handle the ordinary trials of life—sickness, death, financial difficulty, relationship problems, etc. If Paul could endure hunger, thirst, nakedness, beatings, and all the rest with steadfast hope and joy, surely he has something to teach us about how to overcome our comparatively mundane trials.

We get a glimpse of the secret to Paul's magnificent faith in Acts, chapters 19 and 20, as his life was drawing to a close. For over forty years he had been used mightily by the Lord—planting churches, winning people to Christ, discipling them—and his faith had become strong and deep. But in the process, he had gained more enemies than you could shake a stick at. They were everywhere he went, plotting and planning his death. By the time he arrived in Ephesus on his third missionary journey, there was a general sense among the brethren that Paul was a man doomed to this world.

Acts chapter 19 tells us that Paul, Gaius, and Aristarchus were preaching the Gospel in Ephesus, the leading commercial center in the province of Asia and a mecca for worship of the goddess Diana. (The Ephesian temple dedicated to her worship was one of the seven wonders of the ancient world.) The three evangelists were preaching with such power that vast multitudes turned from their pagan idolatry to the Lord. Consequently, the silversmiths who made and sold the little pornographic gods and goddesses used in this demonic activity were actually going out of business! (Wouldn't it be wonderful to experience such a powerful move of the Spirit in our day, causing ungodly businesses to literally close up shop?!)

The Ephesian merchants were infuriated over their loss of income, so they gathered a huge crowd in the center of town, and tried to bring about a revival of Diana worship. For two solid hours they chanted, "Great is Diana of the Ephesians! Great is Diana of the Ephesians!" as they attempted to coerce the new Christians back to their pagan lifestyles.

The silversmiths had seized Gaius and Aristarchus and were holding them in the midst of the mob, but both the local Christians and government officials prevented Paul from getting involved. When it was all over, Paul realized his presence had become a distraction to the ministry, so he left Ephesus and continued his missionary journey. He seemed to sense that the end was drawing near though; so on his way to Jerusalem for the Day of Pentecost, he arranged a meeting with the Ephesian elders in order to pass the baton of leadership to them. He prepares them for his absence, saying,

See, now I go bound in the Spirit to Jerusalem, not knowing the things that will happen to me there, except that the Holy Spirit testifies in every city, saying that chains and tribulations await me.

This is one side of the equation; but then he adds the other side,

But none of these things move me; nor do I count my life dear to myself, so that I may finish my race with joy, and the ministry which I received from the Lord Jesus, to testify to the gospel of the grace of God.

Paul had no fear of the future. In one jam-packed sentence he tells us why and how that was. Thus, he draws for us the blueprint for a triumphant faith.

The next five chapters are devoted to various features from that blueprint. Together we will examine the architecture of Paul's majestic faith and thus learn how to build our own.

APPLICATION & EXHORTATION

1. Do you expect sorrow and pain in this life, or do trials shatter your faith in God?

———❧❧———

For affliction does not come from the dust, nor does trouble spring from the ground; yet man is born to trouble, as the sparks fly upward.

—Job 5:6–7

For His anger is but for a moment, His favor is for life; weeping may endure for a night, but joy comes in the morning.

—Psalm 30:5

These things I have spoken to you, that in Me you may have peace. In the world you will have tribulation; but be of good cheer, I have overcome the world.

—John 16:33

2.   Does your faith in Christ inspire some to believe and others to revile you, or does it inspire no response at all?

———— ❧❦ ————

Now thanks be to God who always leads us in triumph in Christ, and through us diffuses the fragrance of His knowledge in every place. For we are to God the fragrance of Christ among those who are being saved and among those who are perishing. To the one we are the aroma of death leading to death, and to the other the aroma of life leading to life.

—2 Corinthians 2:14–16

Beloved, do not think it strange concerning the fiery trial which is to try you, as though some strange thing happened to you; but rejoice to the extent that you partake of Christ's sufferings, that when His glory is revealed, you may also be glad with exceeding joy. If you are reproached for the name of Christ, blessed are you, for the Spirit of glory and of God rests upon you. On their part He is blasphemed, but on your part He is glorified.

—1 Peter 4:10–14

Nevertheless I have this against you, that you have left your first love. Remember therefore from where you have fallen; repent and do the first works, or else I will come to you quickly and remove your lampstand from its place—unless you repent.

—Revelation 2:4–5

3. Are you bound in the Spirit to follow wherever God leads, no matter the cost?

But this is what I commanded them, saying, "Obey My voice, and I will be your God, and you shall be My people. And walk in all the ways that I have commanded you, that it may be well with you."

—Jeremiah 7:23

My sheep hear My voice, and I know them, and they follow Me.

—John 10:27

Let this mind be in you which was also in Christ Jesus, who, being in the form of God, did not consider it robbery to be equal with God, but made Himself of no reputation, taking the form of a bondservant, and coming in the likeness of men. And being found in appearance as a man, He humbled Himself and became obedient to the point of death, even the death of the cross.

—Philippians 2:5–8

Chapter Two

Is This Going to Move You?

MANY times when Christians are going through a trial, they are actually going through two trials. They not only have the tragedy or tribulation that is in front of them, but there is a second battle they're fighting at the same time. They grapple with the question: "Will my faith outlast this trial?" That complicates matters. Here in Acts 20:24, Paul says, "I only have the struggle of the event because I determined long ago that nothing would move me."

I had been throwing this verse around freely for some time, but it wasn't until after I was married that I was confronted with the reality that I was still easily moved by trials. My wife Jean and I had met at church and had fallen in love. We got married, sold everything we owned, and settled into life at Capernwray Bible School in England. It was such a wonderful time for us. I was young and zealous—thrilled to be studying the Bible five hours a day. We enjoyed stimulating fellowship with people like Alan Redpath and Stewart and Jill Briscoe, among others. Then to top it all off, after we had only been married for a few months, Jean got pregnant. I was ecstatic, praising the Lord effusively: "Oh, thank You God. I can't believe what You're doing. Calling me unto Yourself, wanting to use me. Giving me such a wonderful wife, and now a child. You are so good!" Then Jean had a miscarriage.

Confusion, anger, and doubt descended like a dark cloud over my happiness and for the first time since the car accident, I found myself truly moved. I hadn't known anything like this in three years of walking with the Lord. I really felt like I had God on the ropes. I don't know if you know what I mean, but God had always had me on the ropes; I was always blowing it, always in trouble. Everything so far had been my fault, but now something had happened that I thought was God's fault. It shook me terribly.

At the time, Jean and I were staying at Alan Redpath's house. So one day when my head was spinning, I went for a walk down a long pathway near the house that went over a little bridge and out into the hills. I questioned the Lord about what had happened and about what it meant for the future: "God, why? What have I held back or done wrong? I sold everything I owned. I've come to England to go to Bible college. What is going on here? I know You weren't on vacation. How will I stand before others talking about Your goodness when You let things like this happen for no apparent reason?" I stopped on the bridge and absent-mindedly began throwing pebbles into the creek. Out of nowhere, a voice so clear it almost seemed audible said, "Don, is this going to move you?"

The words hit me broadside and the questions swirling around my mind instantly ceased, but my first response wasn't gratitude. Instead, I got very defensive because I knew exactly where the Lord had gotten those words. He took my verse! Worse yet, He was using it against me! So I responded, "What do You mean, is this going to move me!? I'm not the guy on trial here today. I didn't lose the child. You lost the child!" But God turned it around on me, prodding, "Well, you've been telling everybody that nothing moves you. Didn't you mean it?" And rather than me having Him on the ropes, suddenly I was on the ropes—again!

The Lord knew I was confused and, underneath it all, wondering, "Who am I?" and, "God, do You love me? Where are You, Lord?" He was testing and refining my faith, and above all, warning me, "Don, I want you to know that if this is going to move you off course at this point, you don't stand a chance of making it to the end of your life. If this is so terrible that you can't surrender and yield to Me, you won't make it through what is still ahead of you in your marriage, in your family, and in your ministry." So, embarrassed and humbled, knowing nothing about why that particular trial had come, I made a decision: "No, Lord, this is not going to move me. I'm not going to let it move me."

Every time there is a trial in our lives, the enemy whispers: "You'd better move off course. You'd better look out for yourself. God doesn't love you. God obviously isn't taking care of you. You wouldn't be in this trial if He cared about you. Where is He now, when you really need Him?" I began to learn never to question in the shadows and darkness what God has taught me about Himself in the light. All that I know of His love and His power and His majesty is not up for discussion when a trial comes.

There have been a number of times since that walk in the English countryside when I have almost started down that path of doubt again, but no sooner do I step one foot in that direction than the Lord brings Acts 20:24 to mind. You see, God did eventually give us three great sons. I was angry with God for taking a child. Then I would get upset if the children He gave us misbehaved or had their own struggles in life. If you're a parent, you know exactly what I mean. How many times in your job, in your finances, in your relationships, do situations come along that have no answer? You're as perplexed as anything and yet through it the Lord is wooing you, "Are you going to run? Are we through?" The wonderful thing about the Christian life is that you can honestly predetermine in your own heart that you are not going to run or give up, no matter what happens.

I'm convinced that the only difference between an immature Christian and a mature one is that the mature Christian has had his faith tested. He has been through some trials by fire. The dross has been burned away and there is a purity that radiates from within. The mature Christian knows that one day he is going to receive something more precious than gold—not *as* precious as gold or *almost* as precious as gold—but the most precious thing in all the world: the perfection of his faith.

In 2 Corinthians 6:33, Paul says he served the Lord "in much patience, in tribulations, in needs and distresses, in stripes, in imprisonments, in tumults, in labors, in sleeplessness, in fastings, by purity, by knowledge, by longsuffering, by kindnesses, by the Holy Spirit, by sincere love." Essentially he is saying, "I have been through a lot in my life and what I have found so far is that in every event in all of life, His grace is sufficient for me. He gets me through it all." Thirty years ago, I received a plaque summarizing this simple truth. It says: "The will of God will never lead you where the grace of God cannot keep you."

The Apostle Peter exhorts us to endure trials "that the genuineness of your faith, being much more precious than gold that perishes, though it is tested by fire, may be found to praise, honor, and glory at the revelation of Jesus Christ, whom having not seen you love. Though now you do not see Him, yet believing, you rejoice with joy inexpressible and full of glory, receiving the end of your faith—the salvation of your souls" (1 Peter 1:6-9).

James actually tells us to count it all joy when we enter into various trials, knowing that the testing of our faith produces patience (James 1:2-3). Most of us get excited when we are leaving a trial. James says, "No, get excited when you see it coming! Let it do its work in you!" Like Paul, count not your life dear to yourself.

APPLICATION & EXHORTATION

1. Do you question God's goodness and love when circumstances seem bleak?

———

God is our refuge and strength, a very present help in trouble.

—Psalm 46:1

Cast your burden on the LORD, and He shall sustain you; He shall never permit the righteous to be moved.

—Psalm 55:22

Who shall separate us from the love of Christ? Shall tribulation, or distress, or persecution, or famine, or nakedness, or peril, or sword? As it is written: "For Your sake we are killed all day long; we are accounted as sheep for the slaughter."

Yet in all these things we are more than conquerors through Him who loved us. For I am persuaded that neither death nor life, nor angels nor principalities nor powers, nor things present nor things to come, nor height nor depth, nor any other created thing, shall be able to separate us from the love of God which is in Christ Jesus our Lord.

—Romans 8:35–39

2. Do you resist the testing of your faith, or do you trust God's love in the midst of trial?

———&?———

Behold, happy is the man whom God corrects; therefore do not despise the chastening of the Almighty. For He bruises, but He binds up; He wounds, but His hands make whole.

—Job 5:17–18

The refining pot is for silver and the furnace for gold, but the LORD tests the hearts.

—Proverbs 17:3

Now no chastening seems to be joyful for the present, but painful; nevertheless, afterward it yields the peaceable fruit of righteousness to those who have been trained by it.

—Hebrews 12:11

3. Will you predetermine in your heart that you will not be moved by trials?

———— ❧❧ ————

Though He slay me, yet will I trust Him.

—Job 13:15a

But He knows the way that I take; when He has tested me, I shall come forth as gold. My foot has held fast to His steps; I have kept His way and not turned aside. I have not departed from the commandment of His lips; I have treasured the words of His mouth more than my necessary food.

—Job 23:10–12

And He said to me, "My grace is sufficient for you, for My strength is made perfect in weakness." Therefore most gladly I will rather boast in my infirmities, that the power of Christ may rest upon me. Therefore I take pleasure in infirmities, in reproaches, in needs, in persecutions, in distresses, for Christ's sake. For when I am weak, then I am strong.

—2 Corinthians 12:9–10

Chapter Three

My Life Isn't Dear to Me

WHEN you and I travel, we usually pull out an auto guide to find a hotel. When Paul traveled, he must have said, "Tell me, what are the prisons like in the next city? What kind of whips do they use there? Do they use stones or rods for the beatings?" He was a guy whose life belonged to God. He had abandoned himself so fully to the Lord that he could literally throw himself in harm's way for the sake of the Gospel! I think sometimes we give our lives to God, but we think once we surrender to Him, He becomes this steward—someone who can make our lives wonderful. And He does, but His criteria of "wonderful" is often fundamentally at odds with our own.

Usually when somebody is moved by trials, it's because they're afraid of losing something that is precious to them. Not Paul. What could you do to this guy or take from him? He was entirely single-minded, showing us that the great secret to a triumphant faith is coming to a place where your life, your agenda, your plans, who you are—why you even exist—is no longer dear to you. You're here for God and His glory. You're here to surrender completely to Him and to experience the magnificent life of Christ lived through you.

I've always naively said, "My life isn't dear. You want to take my life, Lord? Take it." I thought that either I would die in some tragedy or I would live a sort of Norman Rockwell existence until I reached a ripe old age. Then my children, grandchildren, and great grandchildren would gather around me for a wonderful birthday celebration. I would bless and hug them all, pray over them, and then go upstairs to sleep and die a peaceful, painless death.

It was a nice fantasy, but I learned a very simple equation back in high school mathematics that has spiritual implications—the whole is equal to the sum of its parts and no part is greater than the whole. So, if I tell God, "My life isn't dear to me," then I'm telling Him that neither is *any part* dear.

In 1996, the Lord gave me a refresher course in fraction equations! I was jogging on my treadmill, trying to lose some weight. I didn't lose any weight, by the way, but I did have a stroke. About seventeen minutes into a twenty-five minute program, I suddenly became very light-headed and almost fainted. Thinking I was simply out-of-shape, I literally said to myself, "You fat slob, just finish it," and I jogged for another eight minutes.

Something had happened though; my eyesight was blurred in my right eye. When I came downstairs, Jean exclaimed, "What happened? Your eye is bright red!" It went from bad to worse, with my vision growing foggier and foggier, until finally, two days later, I went to an ophthalmologist. He put me through a series of tests, and then sat me down and said, "You've had a stroke, and the vision in your right eye is essentially gone." I didn't believe him.

"No, I didn't have a stroke!" I protested.

He insisted, "Yes, you did!"

We went back and forth arguing like that until I finally gave in, "Okay, we'll go with your opinion on the eye. I guess you know a little more about this thing than I do."

What a revelation it was to discover that the Lord might say, "I don't want your whole life right now, I just want your eyeball!"

"Come on, Lord, take it all."

"No, I'm just coming for a piece."

You see, very often God takes a part to test if He honestly has the whole. It has been well said, "Either Christ is Lord *of all* or He isn't Lord *at all*." So if there is any part of your life, or any part of your body, any relationship, location, job, or anything else that is dear to you, then you will be vulnerable to trials. You'll be susceptible to the continual attacks of the enemy, and you will have a spiritual struggle that goes on and on.

Paul said, "I can do all things through Christ who strengthens me" (Philippians 4:13). He didn't just say, "I can do some things," but having learned to be content in every situation, he could audaciously proclaim, "I can be exalted and I can be abased. I can be full or I can be empty. I can be clothed or I can be naked" (see Philippians 4:11–12). A lot of people can only do half. They can only be exalted, they can only be filled, or they can only be clothed. Paul would say, "Oh, that's too bad. How sad that you can't trust Him through the sorrows of life when you could handle it all triumphantly through Christ! Whether He pours it out on you in abundance or He takes it all away, it doesn't have to phase you—*if* you don't hold your life dear."

Alan Redpath used to describe a Christian as "No more than a dead man on furlough." That's how we ought to think. If we want to have stability, to have nothing move us, then we have to be willing to pay the price of death, and we have to be willing to embrace the individual course that God has laid out for each of us.

Application & Exhortation

1. Do you expect God to be like a steward who responds to your every whim, or will you embrace His definition of a wonderful life?

Do not lay up for yourselves treasures on earth, where moth and rust destroy and where thieves break in and steal; but lay up for yourselves treasures in heaven, where neither moth nor rust destroys and where thieves do not break in and steal. For where your treasure is, there your heart will be also.

—Matthew 6:19–21

But we have this treasure in earthen vessels, that the excellence of the power may be of God and not of us. We are hard-pressed on every side, yet not crushed; we are perplexed, but not in despair; persecuted, but not forsaken; struck down, but not destroyed—always carrying about in the body the

---

dying of the Lord Jesus, that the life of Jesus also may be manifested in our body.

—2 Corinthians 4:7–10

2. What are you afraid of losing? Health, life, loved ones, position, material blessing?

Then Jesus said to His disciples, "If anyone desires to come after Me, let him deny himself, and take up his cross, and follow Me. For whoever desires to save his life will lose it, but whoever loses his life for My sake will find it. For what profit is it to a man if he gains the whole world, and loses his own soul? Or what will a man give in exchange for his soul?"

—Matthew 16:24–26

But Jesus answered them, saying, "The hour has come that the Son of Man should be glorified. Most assuredly, I say to you, unless a grain of wheat falls into the ground and dies, it remains alone; but if it dies, it produces much grain."

—John 12:23

Indeed I also count all things loss for the excellence of the knowledge of Christ Jesus my Lord, for whom I have suffered the loss of all things, and count them as rubbish, that I may gain Christ.

—Philippians 3:8

3. Have you learned to be content in all circumstances?

———ഗ൚———

Not that I speak in regard to need, for I have learned in whatever state I am, to be content: I know how to be abased, and I know how to abound. Everywhere and in all things I have learned both to be full and to be hungry, both to abound and to suffer need.

—Philippians 4:11–12

Now godliness with contentment is great gain. For we brought nothing into this world, and it is certain we can carry nothing out.

—1 Timothy 6:6–7

Chapter Four

THAT I MAY FINISH MY COURSE

IN Acts 20:24, Paul told the Ephesian elders that he had a course to finish. Do you know that you have a course ordained by God? Many people don't like their course. They want someone else's course. That's already been tried and it doesn't work! You may remember when Jesus, after His resurrection, told Peter what manner of death he would die, saying, "When you were young, you did what you wanted, but when you're old, it's not going to go so well." Peter didn't like that course, so he looked over at John and said, "What about him? I'll take door number two! Give him door number one; he's a dying sort of a guy!" But Jesus answered, "What difference does it make if I let him live until I come again? I have a course for him, but Peter, here is yours: It may look bad, but I'll be with you and My glory will be revealed in you. Do you trust Me enough to accept your course?" (See John 21.)

When I came on staff at Calvary Chapel Costa Mesa in the early '70s, the revival taking place was reminiscent of Ephesus. Vast multitudes of people were getting saved and the church was always overflowing with people. There were weekly concerts on Saturday and Tuesday nights, with some of the greatest Christian musicians of the day performing. There seemed to be only one event that didn't entirely pack the place out: the Bible study I taught on Friday nights!

I also taught a home Bible study during the week. Members of two popular bands attended, one called "Love Song," and the other, "Children of the Day." Every once in a while these musicians would show up at my Friday night study. They were so encouraging. When they came, they would say, "Don, there's nobody here!"

"Well, there's somebody," I would answer, "There's my wife and the worship leader, so I always have at least two people!"

For some reason they liked me and wanted people to hear me teach, so they offered to alternate weeks performing their music at the Friday night study. It would have been so easy to say "Yes." I would have been guaranteed a huge audience for my messages, but I didn't have peace about it. So I prayed, and then I went to Pastor Chuck Smith for advice. He wasn't much help! He said, "Well, what do you want to do? It's up to you."

I told him, "We have concerts twice a week already and I feel God wants me to keep on with what I'm doing. I'm trying to learn to teach." That was the road for me, so I said "No" to the musicians.

Whatever our course is, we have to determine to embrace it and not covet somebody else's course. Because I had been saved through the ministry of Billy Graham, there was a time when I wanted to be Billy Graham. Unfortunately for me, the job was already taken! Sometimes we have a tendency to romanticize Christian leaders or people like Paul, this phenomenal, godly man. We think, "Oh, how I'd love to have a life so rich and so wonderful." Yet if we stop to consider Paul's life—perils of the land, perils of the sea, perils of the Jews, perils from his countrymen, a night and a day in the deep, five times forty lashes less one, three times beaten with rods—the reality doesn't sound so romantic. We want to be as spiritual as Paul, but are we willing to suffer like Paul to get there? No, not voluntarily!

However, we aren't called to Paul's course. We only have to contend with the course that is ordained for us by God. We have to accept our circumstances, and not be divided about them. Instead, we can thrive in them and thrill in them. I don't know why we lost a child, why we've lost friends over the years, why I lost an eye, or why I'm not Billy Graham, but one thing I do know: What really validates my love for God is if I can trust Him with my course, if I can say "Yes and amen" to whatever flows from His hand.

After my stroke, I had a couple appointments with the ophthalmologist and upon returning home, Jean would ask me to repeat everything the doctor had said. But because I didn't ask a lot of questions, he didn't say a whole lot. So Jean decided to go with me to the next appointment. In the exam room, the ophthalmologist tried to explain to her that the eye was gone. He said, "Don's vision will never get better. The retina is damaged and it will not regenerate itself." But my wife didn't believe him any more than I had. She decided she would teach him something about the art of ophthalmology that he hadn't yet learned! Her argument went something like this: "He's going to lose some weight and start taking vitamins. I'm going to cook better meals for him, and get him to slow down; he's been working too hard. I'll get him to relax more." The doctor wasn't persuaded. Eventually it was as if he had to say to her, "Lady, what does the word *forever* mean to you?"

As this dialogue was going back and forth, I was thinking about Acts 20:24, "... that I might finish my course with joy ..." and here the doctor was telling me a little bit about my course. He had told my wife a few more times that I would never get better, and I was sitting there contemplating this fact when, all of a sudden, I felt as if the Lord was walking me down a hallway, leading me to a door. (It resembled one of those doors on a game show with the prizes behind them!) The words "Never get better" were posted on it. The Lord had a big smile on His face as He opened the door and invited me through. He said, "Here is another path to go down called 'Never Get Better.' Would you like to go with Me?"

I had been down roads that said, "Detour" and "Not now, later," but I had never been down, "Never get better," and the invitation seemed so wonderful—like He was inviting me to Disneyland or something. Ultimately, if we live out a normal life, we're all going to go down a lot of roads that say, "Never get better." So I said, "Lord, I'd be honored to go down that road with You. I want to discover something about You in this event that I wouldn't have otherwise known." It was thrilling.

Paul was willing to go through whatever door the Holy Spirit opened— "Shipwrecked," "Prison," "Exaltation"–he accepted every invitation. And because nothing moved him and because his life wasn't dear to him, he was free in his course to discover what the Lord had for him there that he couldn't have experienced anywhere else. Don't you want to discover the Lord anew through the joys and sorrows of life? Whatever door He opens, take His hand and go through it!

Only a few weeks after my stroke, I attended a baptism at Pirates' Cove Beach in Corona del Mar, California. My depth perception was still pretty bad, and as I navigated the steep set of stairs that descends the cliff leading to the beach, I called out to Jesus to guide me so I wouldn't fall. What followed was the most wonderful walk down that cliff that I had ever taken! His presence guiding and sustaining me was so marvelous. In my weakness, I experienced His strength in a new and powerful way.

A few years later, when I was pastor of a church in San Jose, California, I had a terrible flu that began in October and hung on throughout the winter. Apparently, I was a lot sicker than I realized because one day, at the end of February, I was having lunch at Marie Callender's with an elder from the church when all of a sudden I started spitting up blood. My friend saw the napkin I was coughing into turn bright red, so he said, "Let's get out of here," and threw his money down on the table. We rushed to a nearby urgent care facility, where they checked me out and, inexplicably, sent me home. That night, as I ate dinner, I once again began choking on blood. Jean and I jumped into the car and raced to the hospital. When we arrived, the emergency room staff flew into a panic trying to figure out why I was literally drowning in my own blood. One lung was entirely filled up with blood, and the overflow that I wasn't spitting up or swallowing was pouring into the other lung.

It was a very dramatic scene. Although I was in and out of consciousness, I sensed that this was "it," that before the doctors came up with a solution, I would be gone. It didn't help that as I lay on the table struggling to breathe, doctors and nurses were frantically working to revive a man in the next bed who was having a heart attack. He died. Then, a couple times, my blood pressure and heart rate dropped so low that I actually felt my heart stop and I could feel myself fading away. Even Jean was convinced it was all over. She couldn't believe that what had begun as an ordinary day of shopping and errands might turn out to be our last together here on Earth. I told her I thought I'd lived with an angel for thirty years, and it had been wonderful. She had to remind me of that when I got home!

Somehow the doctors and nurses kept me hanging on until they determined, incorrectly, that a malignant tumor had caused a main artery in my lung to rupture. Emergency surgery was necessary to save my life. I signed all the paperwork, and as they were wheeling me down the hall towards the operating room, the surgeon looked down at me solemnly, and said, "I want you to know we're going to do everything we can."

Already I had been thinking, "Is this going to move me?" and had concluded, "Hey, I've already raised teenagers; come on God, we settled this a long time ago!" Many times we tell the Lord we love Him, but there's nothing on the table, so to speak. We say, "I trust You and I give You my life," but for the most part, it's just a point of discussion. Here I was in a very critical situation, and I had the opportunity to say, "Lord, I've told You in the easy times, the good times, that I love You and I trust You. I want You to know I still love You, and I trust You no matter what happens."

So I looked up at this surgeon who, in one sense, had my life in his hands, and answered, "Well, doc, you go ahead and do your best. If you bring me back, great. But I want you to know that if you don't, it's okay because I'm a Christian. And for me to live is Christ, to die is gain. Absent from the body, I'll be present with the Lord. If you lose me, the best thing in the world will happen to me."

He stared back at me, dumbfounded, and responded, "That's good," like, "Hang on to that thought. That's a winner, baby. I wish all my patients didn't care if they lived or died; it would make practicing medicine so much easier!" I couldn't help but laugh. I grabbed his hand and stopped him, "No, wait a minute, back this up! This isn't good; it's true! I've been getting ready for this moment for thirty years. I just didn't know it might be today. How about you? Are you ready? Do you believe the Gospel message?" He answered, "Well, I believe you believe it, and that's the important thing right now." Satisfied that he understood, I said, "I do and I'll pray for you." We had some good conversations during my recovery.

I lost a section of my right lung that day, but God had brought me to a place where I was able to say I was thrilled in my course; not so much in the pain or the difficulty, but the great adventure was in having only the physical trial in front of me instead of two trials—the physical crisis complicated by a struggle over whether or not I would trust God in the face of death. By His grace I came through able to say it was all right, whether I lived or died.

What a contrast from that walk in the English countryside all those years ago. But that decision I made as a young man to say, "No, Lord, this isn't going to move me" was like laying the first bricks of a sturdy foundation for the future, with every decision after that to respond in faith reinforcing that foundation. That's how it is for every one of us. Then, when the testing of our faith comes, we discover in ever more profound ways that His amazing grace brings peace and joy in the midst of suffering.

APPLICATION & EXHORTATION

1. Are you coveting someone else's course in life or thrilling and thriving in your own?

⸺ഔരു⸺

The LORD is my shepherd; I shall not want.

—Psalm 23:1

But the path of the just is like the shining sun, that shines ever brighter unto the perfect day.

—Proverbs 4:18

Jesus said to him, "Feed My sheep. Most assuredly, I say to you, when you were younger, you girded yourself and walked where you wished; but when you are old, you will stretch out your hands, and another will gird you and carry you where you do not wish." This He spoke, signifying by what death he would glorify God. And when He had spoken this, He said to him, "Follow Me."

—John 21:17b–19

Let your conduct be without covetousness; be content with such things as you have. For He Himself has said, "I will never leave you nor forsake you."

—Hebrews 13:5

2. Are you willing to walk with the Lord through situations that may never get better?

───※───

And lest I should be exalted above measure by the abundance of the revelations, a thorn in the flesh was given to me, a messenger of Satan to buffet me, lest I be exalted above measure.

—2 Corinthians 12:7

The Spirit Himself bears witness with our spirit that we are children of God, and if children, then heirs—heirs of God and joint heirs with Christ, if indeed we suffer with Him, that we may also be glorified together.

—Romans 8:16–17

Do not fear any of those things which you are about to suffer ... be faithful until death, and I will give you the crown of life.

—Revelation 2:10

3. Are you allowing the current trials of life to prepare you for what lies ahead, or are you resisting the Lord's sovereignty?

———❦❧———

Now see that I, even I, am He, and there is no God besides Me; I kill and I make alive; I wound and I heal; nor is there any who can deliver from My hand.

—Deuteronomy 32:39

I know that You can do everything, and that no purpose of Yours can be withheld from You.

—Job 42:2

We also glory in tribulations, knowing that tribulation produces perseverance; and perseverance, character; and character, hope. Now hope does not disappoint, because the love of God has been poured out in our hearts by the Holy Spirit who was given to us.

—Romans 5:3–5

But may the God of all grace, who called us to His eternal glory by Christ Jesus, after you have suffered a while, perfect, establish, strengthen, and settle you.

—1 Peter 5:10

Chapter Five

FINISHING WITH JOY

MANY Christians accept the trials they go through, and they get through them somehow or another, but they do it with misery. They're angry and bitter or they're wounded and suffering: "This is the worst trial!" They make sure everyone knows what God has done to them and everybody's hearts go out to them. They may not quit being Christians over their situations, but they say, "Boy, when I get to Heaven I've got some real questions for God. Yessiree, Bob! He's gonna answer some things for me." What a shame! They say they've given their lives to Christ, but have they?

Paul had no questions. He had absolutely no reservations. When the leaders of Ephesus begged him not to go to Jerusalem, Paul adamantly resisted them, saying, "I beg your pardon, I've been on this course for over forty years. Through every trial, all Jesus does is reveal to me something of Himself that I wouldn't have known unless the trial had come. He reveals to me something of His glory, something of His love, something of His strength and wisdom; and then reveals it through me to others. And you want to keep me from Jerusalem? You've got to be kidding! I won't be denied Jerusalem. It's my course and I am going to enjoy every minute of it. I'll finish it with joy."

I have a suggestion for the Lord. I think there should be a huge arena just outside the entrance gates of Heaven with a sign that says "All Questions Answered Here." It would probably have to hold hundreds of millions of people. I would send a committee of God's friends to answer all the questions people have about their suffering on Earth. I would send people like John the Baptist, who had his head cut off; and Isaiah, who historians believe was sawn in two. I would send Peter, who was crucified upside down; and Stephen, who was stoned to death after he preached his very first sermon. I would send Joseph, who sat in prison for years and years, sold down the creek by his brothers; and Moses, who spent forty years on the backside of the desert babysitting two million murmuring Hebrews. I'd send Hannah, who longed and prayed that God would give her a child; and Naomi, who lost everything that was dear to her when her husband and sons died in a foreign land.

I think just watching these folks walk into the arena would settle most of the questions. Stephen will be the guy who's a little lumpy from being stoned; Peter will be hanging upside down; John will be the guy holding his head in his hands; Isaiah will be the guy who's beside himself! These mutilated heroes of the faith will stumble up to the platform: "Folks, we understand many of you are bitter and angry. We heard you've got some questions."

Can you imagine if one of them came to me and said, "Don, I understand you have a question. Come up here to the microphone"? So, I go up to the mic and stutter, "Uhh, I want to know how come I lost my eyeball?" I can just see it. John would respond: "What? Did he say his eyeball!? He's upset about his eyeball!? Did you hear that, Peter? He must be really blind if he can't see that I had my head chopped off!" I think the whole crowd would be silenced before another person could get up to complain.

Yes, in life there's great sorrow. Think about the death of a child for instance, something that would rip the heart out of any human being. I don't make light of suffering. But these events are the realities of life for which His grace is sufficient, through which His wisdom and His love will bring greater life and greater power and greater victory. The rain falls on the just and the unjust alike, but for those who trust the Lord, there can be unspeakable joy in the midst of our trials!

APPLICATION & EXHORTATION

1. Are you secretly harboring anger or bitterness against the Lord because of your circumstances?

Cease from anger, and forsake wrath; do not fret—it only causes harm.

—Psalm 37:8

Therefore we do not lose heart. Even though our outward man is perishing, yet the inward man is being renewed day by day. For our light affliction, which is but for a moment, is working for us a far more exceeding and eternal weight of glory, while we do not look at the things which are seen, but at the things which are not seen. For the things which are seen are temporary, but the things which are not seen are eternal.

—2 Corinthians 4:16–18

Therefore humble yourselves under the mighty hand of God, that He may exalt you in due time, casting all your care upon Him, for He cares for you.

—1 Peter 5:6–7

2. Wouldn't you rather have joy in the midst of sorrow?

———ΩΩ———

Make me hear joy and gladness, that the bones You have broken may rejoice.

—Psalm 51:8

Those who sow in tears shall reap in joy. He who continually goes forth weeping, bearing seed for sowing, shall doubtless come again with rejoicing, bringing his sheaves with him.

—Psalm 126:5–6

Yet I will rejoice in the LORD, I will joy in the God of my salvation. The LORD God is my strength; He will make my feet like deer's feet, and He will make me walk on my high hills.

—Habakkuk 3:18–19

3. Will you relinquish bitterness now and allow Jesus to fill you with Himself so that you can experience the abundant life He promises?

Surely He has borne our griefs and carried our sorrows; yet we esteemed Him stricken, smitten by God, and afflicted. But He was wounded for our transgressions, He was bruised for our iniquities; the chastisement for our peace was upon Him, and by His stripes we are healed.

—Isaiah 53:4–5

Come, and let us return to the LORD; for He has torn, but He will heal us; He has stricken, but He will bind us up. After two days He will revive us; on the third day He will raise us up, that we may live in His sight.

—Hosea 6:1–2

The thief does not come except to steal, and to kill, and to destroy. I have come that they may have life, and that they may have it more abundantly.

—John 10:10

Now hope does not disappoint, because the love of God has been poured out in our hearts by the Holy Spirit who was given to us.

—Romans 5:5

Chapter Six

To Testify of the Gospel of Jesus Christ

EVERY Christian is alive for one reason—to know Jesus Christ and to make Him known. Paul said, "I finish my course with joy; and, in the process, I get to share Christ wherever I go. When I'm in prison, I get to share Christ. When I'm on the seas, I get to share Christ. And as others can't enjoy the prison, I can show them the secret of enjoying the prison. When we get shipwrecked and everyone is sinking and crying out to their gods who won't deliver them, they turn to me, and say, 'You know, your God seems to give you rest,' and I can introduce them to the source of that rest." In Acts 20:26, Paul declared himself innocent of the blood of all men in Ephesus because he had not failed to preach the Gospel to them. What a bold claim! Would that we could end our days on Earth saying we hadn't failed to turn every situation into an opportunity to know Christ and to make Him known.

In 2 Corinthians 1:3 Paul elaborated on this idea: "Blessed be the God and the Father of our Lord Jesus Christ, the Father of mercies, the God of all comfort, who comforts us in all or our tribulation that we may be able to comfort those who are in any trouble with the comfort with which we ourselves are comforted by God. And as for the sufferings of Christ, they abound in us, so our consolation also abounds in Christ." Paul could speak with authority because of the trials he went through.

Don't you want to be like this amazing man who lived through so much and seemed to do it so gallantly, so royally, with such triumph in his life? It begins with a decision not to be moved, or to hold anything dear, or to covet anyone else's course, but instead to abandon yourself to Christ so He can fill you with peace, hope, joy, and a message for others.

APPLICATION & EXHORTATION

1. Do you view your suffering as an opportunity to know Christ and make Him known?

—————— ✿ ——————

I have heard of You by the hearing of the ear, but now my eye sees You.

—Job 42:5

But I want you to know, brethren, that the things which happened to me have actually turned out for the furtherance of the gospel.

—Philippians 1:12

2. Can you say with Paul that you have not failed to turn every situation into an opportunity for the Gospel to be proclaimed?

But as for you, you meant evil against me; but God meant it for good, in order to bring it about as it is this day, to save many people alive.

—Genesis 50:20

And we know that all things work together for good to those who love God, to those who are the called according to His purpose.

—Romans 8:28

3. Will you ask the Lord today to empower you with a bold faith that turns every experience into a tool for the furtherance of His kingdom?

———— ✠✠ ————

But you shall receive power when the Holy Spirit has come upon you; and you shall be witnesses to Me in Jerusalem, and in all Judea and Samaria, and to the end of the earth.

—Acts 1:8

Therefore, my beloved brethren, be steadfast, immovable, always abounding in the work of the Lord, knowing that your labor is not in vain in the Lord.

—1 Corinthians 15:58

FINAL EXHORTATION

MAYBE today there is something dear to you, something you think you can't live without. Then you're a trial waiting to happen. Maybe God is saying to you, "Give it up." The whole is equal to the sum of its parts, so give it up! Want to finish well? Then determine that you will. You can do all things through Him who gives you strength.

All the trials of life are really His graces. When I thought He took a child, He gave grace. When I thought He took an eye, He gave grace. When He took a lung, He gave more grace. Whenever He's taking, He gives back so much more. But if you won't take the grace He has to give, you'll be stuck grasping for whatever is being taken, and you'll be bitter. And what does bitterness do, but destroy everything that's good in your life? You still have to contend with the suffering and sorrow, and then you have misery besides. Who wants that when you can know Him and make Him known through all of life's challenges?

I pray Jesus would spoil you with His presence, that you would realize that the sufferings of the present aren't even worthy to be compared with the glory that shall be revealed. I pray that we could get on with it, every one of us, and say, "I'm going to finish my course with joy. No more anger, no more questions, no more bitterness. I want to discover the comfort of God, the power, the love, the blessing, the hope—that I may finish with joy in the ministry that I have received of the Lord Jesus to testify of who He is, and how wonderful it is to have Him leading me on my course." Amen!

ABOUT THE AUTHOR

DON McClure came to Christ at a Billy Graham Los Angeles Crusade in the 1960s. While completing his Bachelor of Science degree in Business Administration at Cal Poly Pomona, he sensed the call of God on his life to enter full-time ministry. He subsequently met Alan Redpath who invited him to England, where he attended Capernwray Bible School. Upon returning to the United States, he continued his studies at Talbot Seminary in La Mirada, California.

Early in Don's ministry, he served for four years as an assistant pastor to Chuck Smith at Calvary Chapel of Costa Mesa, California. Next Don pioneered and pastored a church in Lake Arrowhead, California, for four years. He also founded Calvary Chapel Bible College in nearby Twin Peaks at the Calvary Chapel Conference Center. Sensing the Lord's direction to move on, Don pioneered and pastored another Calvary Chapel in Redlands, California, for eleven years. In 1991, Don began serving as senior pastor of Calvary Chapel San Jose, California. And, in September 2002, Don returned to Calvary Chapel of Costa Mesa to serve as an associate pastor to Chuck Smith.

Don has been instrumental in establishing Calvary Chapels across the country. He has a passion for evangelism, church planting, teaching the Word, and the development and training of leaders within the Body of Christ.

Don's teaching is practical, encouraging, inspirational, and challenging. His radio ministry, "The Calvary Way," can be heard weekdays on KWave, 107.9 FM. He can also be heard live on the Internet @ www.kwve.org.

Don and his wife, Jean, have been married for thirty-five years. They have three sons and five grandchildren.